About Skill Builders

Multiplication and Division

Grades 4–5

Welcome to Skill Builders *Multiplication and Division* for grades 4–5. This book is designed to improve children's multiplication and division skills through focused practice. This full-color workbook contains grade-level-appropriate activities based on national standards to help ensure that children master basic skills before progressing.

More than 70 pages of activities cover essential skills such as problem solving, multiplying and dividing whole numbers, and multiplying and dividing fractions and decimals. The book's colorful, inviting format, easy-to-follow directions, and clear examples help build children's confidence and make math more accessible and enjoyable.

The Skill Builders series offers workbooks that are perfect for keeping skills sharp during the school year or preparing students for the next grade.

www.carsondellosa.com
Carson-Dellosa Publishing LLC
Greensboro, North Carolina

ISBN 978-1-936023-29-5
02-150111151

Table of Contents

Multiplication Facts Review, 1–6

Complete the table. Then, answer the questions.

×	1	2	3	4	5	6
1						
2						
3						
4						
5						
6						

1. What does any number times 1 equal?

2. What pattern do you see in the 2s?

3. What pattern do you see in the 5s?

4. Are all the numbers you multiplied by 2 odd or even?

5. $3 \times 4 = 12$. What does 4×3 equal?

Multiplication Facts Review, 7–12

Complete the table. Then, answer the questions.

×	7	8	9	10	11	12
7						
8						
9						
10						
11						
12						

1. When you multiply 9 by a single-digit number, add the digits in the answer. What do they equal?

2. When you multiply a number by ten, what is in the ones place of the product?

3. When you multiply 11 by a single-digit number, what is the result?

Associative Property of Multiplication

Complete each equation using the Associative Property.

> The **Associative Property of Multiplication** states that changing the grouping of factors does not change the product.
>
> **Example:**
>
> $$(4 \times 3) \times 2 = 24 \qquad 4 \times (3 \times 2) = 24$$

1. $(18 \times 0) \times 6 =$ _____ $\times ($ _____ $\times$ _____ $)$

2. $6 \times (3 \times 4) = ($ _____ $\times$ _____ $) \times$ _____

3. $(8 \times 7) \times 6 =$ _____ $\times ($ _____ $\times$ _____ $)$

4. $6 \times (12 \times 12) = ($ _____ $\times$ _____ $) \times$ _____

5. $(6 \times 7) \times 4 = 6 \times ($ _____ $\times$ _____ $)$

6. $9 \times (5 \times 5) = ($ _____ $\times$ _____ $) \times$ _____

7. _____ $\times ($ _____ $\times$ _____ $) = (0 \times 4) \times 6$

8. $(5 \times 6) \times 9 =$ _____ $\times (6 \times$ _____ $)$

9. $(241 \times 1) \times 1 =$ _____ $\times (1 \times 1)$

10. $9 \times (4 \times 3) = ($ _____ $\times$ _____ $) \times$ _____

11. $3 \times (12 \times 10) = ($ _____ $\times$ _____ $) \times$ _____

Commutative Property of Multiplication

Complete the pairs of related facts.

$2 \times 4 = \underline{\ \textbf{8}\ }$ so $4 \times 2 = \underline{\ \textbf{8}\ }$

1. $5 \times 3 = \underline{\quad}$ so $3 \times 5 = \underline{\quad}$

2. $1 \times 6 = \underline{\quad}$ so $6 \times 1 = \underline{\quad}$

3. $2 \times 5 = \underline{\quad}$ so $5 \times 2 = \underline{\quad}$

4. $7 \times 3 = \underline{\quad}$ so $3 \times 7 = \underline{\quad}$

5. $3 \times 11 = \underline{\quad}$ so $11 \times 3 = \underline{\quad}$

6. $2 \times 9 = \underline{\quad}$ so $9 \times 2 = \underline{\quad}$

7. $4 \times 6 = \underline{\quad}$ so $6 \times 4 = \underline{\quad}$

8. $2 \times 7 = \underline{\quad}$ so $7 \times 2 = \underline{\quad}$

9. $3 \times 10 = \underline{\quad}$ so $10 \times 3 = \underline{\quad}$

10. $8 \times 2 = \underline{\quad}$ so $2 \times 8 = \underline{\quad}$

11. $12 \times 5 = \underline{\quad}$ so $5 \times 12 = \underline{\quad}$

Multiplying Multiples of 10

Solve the problems. Look for a pattern.

$$\begin{array}{r} 20 \\ \times\ 10 \\ \hline \mathbf{200} \end{array}$$

1. $\begin{array}{r} 30 \\ \times\ 10 \\ \hline \end{array}$

2. $\begin{array}{r} 40 \\ \times\ 10 \\ \hline \end{array}$

3. $\begin{array}{r} 50 \\ \times\ 10 \\ \hline \end{array}$

4. $\begin{array}{r} 60 \\ \times\ 10 \\ \hline \end{array}$

5. $\begin{array}{r} 20 \\ \times\ 20 \\ \hline \end{array}$

6. $\begin{array}{r} 30 \\ \times\ 20 \\ \hline \end{array}$

7. $\begin{array}{r} 40 \\ \times\ 20 \\ \hline \end{array}$

8. $\begin{array}{r} 50 \\ \times\ 20 \\ \hline \end{array}$

9. $\begin{array}{r} 60 \\ \times\ 20 \\ \hline \end{array}$

10. $\begin{array}{r} 30 \\ \times\ 30 \\ \hline \end{array}$

11. $\begin{array}{r} 40 \\ \times\ 30 \\ \hline \end{array}$

12. $\begin{array}{r} 50 \\ \times\ 30 \\ \hline \end{array}$

13. $\begin{array}{r} 60 \\ \times\ 30 \\ \hline \end{array}$

14. $\begin{array}{r} 70 \\ \times\ 30 \\ \hline \end{array}$

Estimation and Multiplication

Estimate first; then multiply to find the answer.

$$\overset{2}{35} \rightarrow 40 \\ \underline{\times 5} \quad \underline{\times 5}$$

Estimate $\underline{\quad 200 \quad}$

Multiply $\underline{\quad 175 \quad}$

1. 18
   $\underline{\times 6}$

2. 41
   $\underline{\times 7}$

3. 29
   $\underline{\times 4}$

---

4. 24
   $\underline{\times 8}$

5. 25
   $\underline{\times 9}$

6. 63
   $\underline{\times 5}$

7. 94
   $\underline{\times 6}$

Estimate

Multiply

---

8. 112
   $\underline{\times 6}$

9. 107
   $\underline{\times 9}$

10. 206
    $\underline{\times 5}$

11. 410
    $\underline{\times 8}$

Estimate

Multiply

2-Digit by 1-Digit Multiplication

Solve each problem.

1. $\begin{array}{r} 12 \\ \times\ 4 \\ \hline \end{array}$ 2. $\begin{array}{r} 11 \\ \times\ 2 \\ \hline \end{array}$ 3. $\begin{array}{r} 13 \\ \times\ 2 \\ \hline \end{array}$ 4. $\begin{array}{r} 13 \\ \times\ 3 \\ \hline \end{array}$ 5. $\begin{array}{r} 14 \\ \times\ 1 \\ \hline \end{array}$

6. $\begin{array}{r} 11 \\ \times\ 3 \\ \hline \end{array}$ 7. $\begin{array}{r} 14 \\ \times\ 2 \\ \hline \end{array}$ 8. $\begin{array}{r} 12 \\ \times\ 3 \\ \hline \end{array}$ 9. $\begin{array}{r} 11 \\ \times\ 4 \\ \hline \end{array}$ 10. $\begin{array}{r} 23 \\ \times\ 3 \\ \hline \end{array}$

11. $\begin{array}{r} 13 \\ \times\ 1 \\ \hline \end{array}$ 12. $\begin{array}{r} 11 \\ \times\ 6 \\ \hline \end{array}$ 13. $\begin{array}{r} 22 \\ \times\ 3 \\ \hline \end{array}$ 14. $\begin{array}{r} 32 \\ \times\ 2 \\ \hline \end{array}$ 15. $\begin{array}{r} 44 \\ \times\ 2 \\ \hline \end{array}$

2-Digit by 1-Digit Multiplication with Regrouping

Solve each problem.

$$
\begin{array}{r}
^{4}\,17 \\
\times\ 7 \\
\hline
\mathbf{119}
\end{array}
$$

1.
$$
\begin{array}{r}
19 \\
\times\ 7 \\
\hline
\end{array}
$$

2.
$$
\begin{array}{r}
23 \\
\times\ 7 \\
\hline
\end{array}
$$

3.
$$
\begin{array}{r}
46 \\
\times\ 7 \\
\hline
\end{array}
$$

4.
$$
\begin{array}{r}
37 \\
\times\ 7 \\
\hline
\end{array}
$$

5.
$$
\begin{array}{r}
63 \\
\times\ 8 \\
\hline
\end{array}
$$

6.
$$
\begin{array}{r}
21 \\
\times\ 8 \\
\hline
\end{array}
$$

7.
$$
\begin{array}{r}
92 \\
\times\ 8 \\
\hline
\end{array}
$$

8.
$$
\begin{array}{r}
83 \\
\times\ 8 \\
\hline
\end{array}
$$

9.
$$
\begin{array}{r}
47 \\
\times\ 8 \\
\hline
\end{array}
$$

10.
$$
\begin{array}{r}
84 \\
\times\ 9 \\
\hline
\end{array}
$$

11.
$$
\begin{array}{r}
27 \\
\times\ 9 \\
\hline
\end{array}
$$

12.
$$
\begin{array}{r}
90 \\
\times\ 9 \\
\hline
\end{array}
$$

13.
$$
\begin{array}{r}
57 \\
\times\ 9 \\
\hline
\end{array}
$$

14.
$$
\begin{array}{r}
75 \\
\times\ 9 \\
\hline
\end{array}
$$

3-Digit by 1-Digit Multiplication with Regrouping

Solve each problem.

Multiply 4 ones by 3. Regroup.	Multiply 2 tens by 3. Add the 1 ten.	Multiply 3 hundreds by 3.
$3\overset{1}{2}4$ $\times\quad3$ $\quad2$	$3\overset{1}{2}4$ $\times\quad3$ $\;72$	$3\overset{1}{2}4$ $\times\quad3$ $\mathbf{9}72$

1. 311
    × 8

2. 248
    × 2

3. 225
    × 4

4. 283
    × 3

5. 143
    × 7

6. 215
    × 3

7. 103
    × 8

8. 150
    × 5

9. 999
    × 2

10. 274
    × 2

11. 103
    × 9

12. 208
    × 4

13. 401
    × 9

14. 210
    × 4

15. 252
    × 3

16. 200
    × 6

4-Digit by 1-Digit Multiplication with Regrouping

Solve each problem.

Multiply 9 ones by 2. Regroup.	Multiply 2 tens by 2. Remember to add the 1.	Multiply 1 hundred by 2.	Multiply 5 thousands by 2.
$5,12\overset{1}{2}9$ $\times\ \ \ \ \ 2$ $\overline{\qquad\ 8}$	$5,1\overset{1}{2}9$ $\times\ \ \ \ \ 2$ $\overline{\ \ \ 5\,8}$	$5,\mathbf{1}\overset{1}{2}9$ $\times\ \ \ \ \ 2$ $\overline{\ 2\,5\,8}$	$\mathbf{5},1\overset{1}{2}9$ $\times\ \ \ \ \ 2$ $\overline{\mathbf{10},258}$

1. 2,000
    × 3

2. 3,000
    × 3

3. 2,110
    × 4

4. 3,021
    × 2

5. 4,210
    × 3

6. 3,145
    × 2

7. 2,041
    × 4

8. 5,120
    × 6

9. 6,814
    × 2

10. 8,521
    × 3

2-, 3-, and 4-Digit by 1-Digit Multiplication: Problem Solving

Solve each problem.

1. Jan drove 843 miles. Rex drove 4 times as many miles as Jan. How many miles did Rex drive?

   _____

2. The Blueline train is 5 times farther from Jake's house than the Redline train. The Redline is 2,300 yards from Jake's house. How far from Jake's house is the Blueline?

   _____

3. Jeff drove 98 laps around the racetrack. If the racetrack is 3 miles long, how many miles did Jeff drive?

   _____

4. Mark traveled 1,694 miles on his vacation. Susan traveled 3 times as many miles as Mark. How many miles did Susan travel?

   _____

5. If Amanda drove 65 miles per hour, how far did she drive in 7 hours?

   _____

6. Tony drove 543 miles farther than Patrick. Patrick drove 8 times as many miles as Jeff. If Jeff drove 296 miles, how far did Tony drive? How far did Patrick drive?

   _____

2-Digit by 2-Digit Multiplication with Regrouping

Solve each problem.

Multiply 34 by 8 ones.	Multiply 34 by 1 ten.	Add.
$\begin{array}{r} 3\,4 \\ \times\,1\,8 \\ \hline 2\,7\,2 \end{array}$	$\begin{array}{r} 3\,4 \\ \times\,1\,8 \\ \hline 2\,7\,2 \\ +\,3\,4\,0 \end{array}$	$\begin{array}{r} 3\,4 \\ \times\,1\,8 \\ \hline 2\,7\,2 \\ +\,3\,4\,0 \\ \hline 6\,1\,2 \end{array}$

1. $\begin{array}{r} 56 \\ \times\,35 \\ \hline \end{array}$

2. $\begin{array}{r} 37 \\ \times\,12 \\ \hline \end{array}$

3. $\begin{array}{r} 91 \\ \times\,37 \\ \hline \end{array}$

4. $\begin{array}{r} 64 \\ \times\,34 \\ \hline \end{array}$

5. $\begin{array}{r} 29 \\ \times\,43 \\ \hline \end{array}$

6. $\begin{array}{r} 24 \\ \times\,83 \\ \hline \end{array}$

7. $\begin{array}{r} 13 \\ \times\,24 \\ \hline \end{array}$

8. $\begin{array}{r} 24 \\ \times\,32 \\ \hline \end{array}$

9. $\begin{array}{r} 15 \\ \times\,23 \\ \hline \end{array}$

10. $\begin{array}{r} 18 \\ \times\,23 \\ \hline \end{array}$

11. $\begin{array}{r} 34 \\ \times\,52 \\ \hline \end{array}$

12. $\begin{array}{r} 43 \\ \times\,24 \\ \hline \end{array}$

3-Digit by 2-Digit Multiplication with Regrouping

Solve each problem.

Multiply 612 by 7 ones.	Multiply 612 by 3 tens.	Add.
$\begin{array}{r} 6\,1\,2 \\ \times\quad 3\,7 \\ \hline 4,2\,8\,4 \end{array}$	$\begin{array}{r} 6\,1\,2 \\ \times\quad 3\,7 \\ \hline 4,2\,8\,4 \\ 1\,8,3\,6\,0 \end{array}$	$\begin{array}{r} 6\,1\,2 \\ \times\quad 3\,7 \\ \hline 4,2\,8\,4 \\ +\,1\,8,3\,6\,0 \\ \hline 2\,2,6\,4\,4 \end{array}$

1. $\begin{array}{r} 541 \\ \times\ 82 \\ \hline \end{array}$

2. $\begin{array}{r} 219 \\ \times\ 20 \\ \hline \end{array}$

3. $\begin{array}{r} 375 \\ \times\ 94 \\ \hline \end{array}$

4. $\begin{array}{r} 511 \\ \times\ 40 \\ \hline \end{array}$

5. $\begin{array}{r} 357 \\ \times\ 49 \\ \hline \end{array}$

6. $\begin{array}{r} 125 \\ \times\ 12 \\ \hline \end{array}$

7. $\begin{array}{r} 478 \\ \times\ 39 \\ \hline \end{array}$

8. $\begin{array}{r} 324 \\ \times\ 35 \\ \hline \end{array}$

9. $\begin{array}{r} 127 \\ \times\ 32 \\ \hline \end{array}$

10. $\begin{array}{r} 461 \\ \times\ 63 \\ \hline \end{array}$

11. $\begin{array}{r} 214 \\ \times\ 28 \\ \hline \end{array}$

12. $\begin{array}{r} 513 \\ \times\ 41 \\ \hline \end{array}$

4-Digit by 2-Digit Multiplication with Regrouping

Solve each problem.

	Multiply 1,249 by 2 ones.	Multiply 1,249 by 3 tens.	Add.
$\begin{array}{r} 1,249 \\ \times\ \ \ 32 \\ \hline \end{array}$	$\begin{array}{r} {}^{1}\ \ \ \\ 1,249 \\ \times\ \ \ 32 \\ \hline 2,498 \end{array}$	$\begin{array}{r} {}^{1}\ {}^{2}\ \\ {}_{1}\ \\ 1,249 \\ \times\ \ \ 32 \\ \hline 2,498 \\ 37,470 \end{array}$	$\begin{array}{r} {}^{1}\ {}^{2}\ \\ {}_{1}\ \\ 1,249 \\ \times\ \ \ 32 \\ \hline 2,498 \\ +\ 37,470 \\ \hline 39,968 \end{array}$

1. $\begin{array}{r} 4,000 \\ \times\ \ \ 10 \\ \hline \end{array}$

2. $\begin{array}{r} 3,000 \\ \times\ \ \ 20 \\ \hline \end{array}$

3. $\begin{array}{r} 8,000 \\ \times\ \ \ 30 \\ \hline \end{array}$

4. $\begin{array}{r} 6,000 \\ \times\ \ \ 60 \\ \hline \end{array}$

5. $\begin{array}{r} 5,000 \\ \times\ \ \ 30 \\ \hline \end{array}$

6. $\begin{array}{r} 6,000 \\ \times\ \ \ 40 \\ \hline \end{array}$

7. $\begin{array}{r} 7,000 \\ \times\ \ \ 30 \\ \hline \end{array}$

8. $\begin{array}{r} 8,000 \\ \times\ \ \ 40 \\ \hline \end{array}$

9. $\begin{array}{r} 3,028 \\ \times\ \ \ 41 \\ \hline \end{array}$

10. $\begin{array}{r} 5,413 \\ \times\ \ \ 23 \\ \hline \end{array}$

11. $\begin{array}{r} 2,135 \\ \times\ \ \ 16 \\ \hline \end{array}$

12. $\begin{array}{r} 4,361 \\ \times\ \ \ 34 \\ \hline \end{array}$

13. $\begin{array}{r} 6,179 \\ \times\ \ \ 82 \\ \hline \end{array}$

14. $\begin{array}{r} 1,349 \\ \times\ \ \ 64 \\ \hline \end{array}$

15. $\begin{array}{r} 4,564 \\ \times\ \ \ 41 \\ \hline \end{array}$

16. $\begin{array}{r} 5,347 \\ \times\ \ \ 35 \\ \hline \end{array}$

4-Digit by 3-Digit Multiplication with Regrouping

Solve each problem.

Multiply 3,214 by 2 ones.	Multiply 3,214 by 4 tens.	Multiply 3,214 by 6 hundreds.	Add.
3,214 × 64**2** 6,428	¹ 3,214 × 6**4**2 6,428 128,560	¹ ² ¹ 3,214 × **6**42 6,428 128,560 1,928,400	¹ ² ¹ 3,214 × 642 **6,428** **128,560** **+1,928,400** **2,063,388**

1. 3,116
   × 200

2. 5,262
   × 300

3. 1,624
   × 700

4. 2,561
   × 400

5. 4,513
   × 124

6. 2,216
   × 320

7. 5,321
   × 124

8. 1,262
   × 414

9. 6,206
   × 417

10. 5,354
    × 124

11. 2,513
    × 216

12. 3,618
    × 407

Multiplying Large Numbers: Problem Solving

Find the number of pages each book club member has read. Use the table to help organize the information.

Caroline read 23 times as many pages as Matt.

Matt read half as many pages as Alicia.

Julie read 346 pages more than Greg.

Greg read 1,598 pages fewer than Caroline.

Alicia read 382 pages.

Becky read twice as many pages as Greg.

Jeff read 15 times as many pages as Alicia.

Name	Pages Read
1. Caroline	
2. Matt	
3. Julie	
4. Greg	
5. Alicia	
6. Becky	
7. Jeff	

Multiplication Review

Solve each problem.

1. $\begin{array}{r} 92 \\ \times\ 3 \\ \hline \end{array}$ 2. $\begin{array}{r} 13 \\ \times\ 4 \\ \hline \end{array}$ 3. $\begin{array}{r} 517 \\ \times\ 7 \\ \hline \end{array}$ 4. $\begin{array}{r} 326 \\ \times\ 5 \\ \hline \end{array}$

5. $\begin{array}{r} 67 \\ \times\ 91 \\ \hline \end{array}$ 6. $\begin{array}{r} 36 \\ \times\ 29 \\ \hline \end{array}$ 7. $\begin{array}{r} 527 \\ \times\ 41 \\ \hline \end{array}$ 8. $\begin{array}{r} 768 \\ \times\ 24 \\ \hline \end{array}$

9. $\begin{array}{r} 8{,}191 \\ \times\ 3 \\ \hline \end{array}$ 10. $\begin{array}{r} 6{,}517 \\ \times\ 5 \\ \hline \end{array}$ 11. $\begin{array}{r} 3{,}271 \\ \times\ 48 \\ \hline \end{array}$ 12. $\begin{array}{r} 6{,}907 \\ \times\ 82 \\ \hline \end{array}$

13. Jack does 15 sit-ups every day for 365 days. How many total sit-ups does he do?

_____

14. Bonnie consumes 1,800 calories every day for 21 days. How many total calories does she consume?

_____

Division Facts Review

Solve each problem.

1. $9\overline{)72}$ 2. $6\overline{)12}$ 3. $8\overline{)40}$ 4. $2\overline{)4}$ 5. $4\overline{)28}$

6. $5\overline{)20}$ 7. $9\overline{)0}$ 8. $6\overline{)6}$ 9. $7\overline{)35}$ 10. $8\overline{)72}$

11. $9\overline{)27}$ 12. $7\overline{)56}$ 13. $3\overline{)27}$ 14. $2\overline{)14}$ 15. $3\overline{)18}$

16. Barry makes $3.00 for every bag of leaves that he rakes. He made $36.00. How many bags of leaves did he rake?

_____

17. Sara's chorus learns 24 new songs in 6 weeks. If they learn the same number of songs per week, how many new songs do they learn each week?

_____

Division Facts Review

Solve each problem.

1. $27 \div 3 =$ 2. $10 \div 2 =$ 3. $12 \div 3 =$ 4. $24 \div 3 =$

5. $0 \div 5 =$ 6. $20 \div 5 =$ 7. $48 \div 6 =$ 8. $5 \div 1 =$

9. $2\overline{)14}$ 10. $9\overline{)81}$ 11. $7\overline{)56}$ 12. $1\overline{)4}$ 13. $7\overline{)63}$

14. $8\overline{)32}$ 15. $6\overline{)42}$ 16. $2\overline{)16}$ 17. $8\overline{)48}$ 18. $3\overline{)9}$

Division Facts (Inverse of Multiplication)

Use the information given to solve each problem.

If...	Then...
$2 \times 3 = 6$	$6 \div 2 = \mathbf{3}$
$3 \times 2 = 6$	$6 \div 3 = \mathbf{2}$

1. $3 \times 2 = 6$
   $6 \div 3 = $ _____

2. $3 \times 3 = 9$
   $9 \div 3 = $ _____

3. $2 \times 4 = 8$
   $8 \div 2 = $ _____

4. $7 \times 1 = 7$
   $7 \div 7 = $ _____

5. $5 \times 0 = 0$
   $0 \div 5 = $ _____

6. $4 \times 5 = 20$
   $20 \div 4 = $ _____

7. $6 \times 3 = 18$
   $18 \div 6 = $ _____

8. $4 \times 3 = 12$
   $12 \div 4 = $ _____

9. $6 \times 6 = 36$
   $36 \div 6 = $ _____

10. $2 \times 5 = 10$
    $10 \div 2 = $ _____

11. $2 \times 7 = 14$
    $14 \div 2 = $ _____

12. $4 \times 9 = 36$
    $36 \div 4 = $ _____

13. $7 \times 3 = 21$
    $21 \div 7 = $ _____

14. $6 \times 8 = 48$
    $48 \div 6 = $ _____

15. $5 \times 5 = 25$
    $25 \div 5 = $ _____

Dividing Multiples of 10

Try doing these problems in your mind. Then, check yourself with a calculator.

These problems work similarly to dividing by 10. You can cancel the zero and focus on a basic fact.

Example:

$$30\overline{)60}$$

$$\begin{array}{r} 2 \\ 30\overline{)60} \\ -60 \\ \hline 0 \end{array}$$

Think: $6 \div 3 = 2$
Place the 2 above the 0, multiply, and subtract.

These problems can usually be worked out in your mind instead of writing the whole algorithm.

1. $40\overline{)80}$

2. $30\overline{)90}$

3. $20\overline{)40}$

4. $40\overline{)40}$

5. $10\overline{)60}$

6. $20\overline{)80}$

Division and Estimation

Estimate which number from within each rectangle would be the correct quotient. Circle the answer.

When dividing by two-digit divisors, begin by trying to divide into the first two digits of the dividend. If this number is not big enough, use the first three digits. Estimate how many times the divisor can go into that number. Then, multiply and subtract. Remember, if the difference is the same as or greater than the divisor, try a larger number in the quotient.

Example:

$$\begin{array}{r} 5 \\ 23\overline{)138} \\ -115 \\ \hline 23 \end{array} \qquad \begin{array}{r} 6 \\ 23\overline{)138} \\ -138 \\ \hline 0 \end{array}$$

The difference is the same as the divisor. Try again.

1. $63\overline{)189}$

$\boxed{3, 4, 5}$

2. $57\overline{)228}$

$\boxed{3, 4, 5}$

3. $56\overline{)336}$

$\boxed{4, 5, 6}$

4. $84\overline{)588}$

$\boxed{5, 6, 7}$

5. $37\overline{)296}$

$\boxed{7, 8, 9}$

6. $19\overline{)171}$

$\boxed{7, 8, 9}$

7. $21\overline{)168}$

$\boxed{6, 7, 8}$

8. $84\overline{)252}$

$\boxed{2, 3, 4}$

2-Digit by 1-Digit Division without Remainders

Solve the following problems.

Example:

$$\begin{array}{r} 13 \\ 6\overline{)78} \\ -6\downarrow \\ \hline 18 \\ -18 \\ \hline 0 \end{array}$$

Long division uses multiple math operations, like multiplying, place value, subtracting, and dividing. You write the **algorithm** to show your steps.

1. $6\overline{)36}$

2. $3\overline{)21}$

3. $5\overline{)75}$

4. $4\overline{)64}$

5. $8\overline{)88}$

6. $7\overline{)56}$

7. $4\overline{)48}$

8. $2\overline{)64}$

9. $5\overline{)65}$

10. $3\overline{)51}$

2-Digit by 1-Digit Division with Remainders

Solve each problem.

Sometimes when you try to divide a number of objects into groups of equal size, you have some objects left over. The number of objects left over is called the **remainder**.

Examples:

$$\begin{array}{r} 5 \\ 4\overline{)20} \\ -20 \\ \hline 0 \end{array}$$ (No remainder)

$$\begin{array}{r} 5\ R2 \\ 4\overline{)22} \\ -20 \\ \hline 2 \end{array}$$ (A remainder)

Example:

$$4\overline{)6}$$

One group of 4 hearts with 2 hearts left over

$$\text{So: } \begin{array}{r} 1\ R2 \\ 4\overline{)6} \\ -4 \\ \hline 2 \end{array}$$

1. $8\overline{)9}$

♥♥♥♥♥
♥♥♥♥

2. $3\overline{)8}$

♥♥♥♥
♥♥♥♥

3. $3\overline{)10}$

♥♥♥
♥♥♥
♥♥♥♥

4. $2\overline{)7}$

♥♥♥♥
♥♥♥

5. $5\overline{)9}$

♥♥♥
♥♥♥
♥♥♥

6. $9\overline{)20}$

♥♥♥♥♥
♥♥♥♥♥
♥♥♥♥♥
♥♥♥♥♥

3-Digit by 1-Digit Division with Remainders

Solve for the quotients.

Keep following the same long division steps, but at the end, make sure your remainder is smaller than the divisor.

Example:

$$
\begin{array}{r}
175 \text{ R1} \\
3\overline{)526} \\
-3\downarrow \\
\overline{22} \\
-21\downarrow \\
\overline{16} \\
-15 \\
\overline{1}
\end{array}
$$

1. $2\overline{)357}$

2. $4\overline{)975}$

3. $5\overline{)823}$

4. $5\overline{)348}$

5. $7\overline{)439}$

6. $8\overline{)591}$

4-Digit by 1-Digit Division with Remainders

Solve each problem.

Example:

$$7\overline{)4{,}359} \quad \mathbf{622\ R5}$$

$\underline{-42}$ ←——— **7 × 6 = 42**

15   Subtract 42 from 43. Bring down the 5.

$\underline{-14}$ ←——— **7 × 2 = 14**

19   Subtract 14 from 15. Bring down the 9.

$\underline{-14}$ ←——— **7 × 2 = 14**

5   Subtract 14 from 19. Because 5 is less than 7, the remainder is 5.

1. $5\overline{)3{,}571}$ 2. $4\overline{)3{,}691}$ 3. $7\overline{)7{,}198}$

4. $2\overline{)8{,}617}$ 5. $3\overline{)2{,}794}$ 6. $4\overline{)6{,}433}$

7. $5\overline{)3{,}127}$ 8. $6\overline{)1{,}467}$ 9. $8\overline{)6{,}959}$

2-, 3-, and 4-Digit by 1-Digit Division Word Problems

Solve each problem.

1. There are 45 reptiles at the zoo. Altogether, there are the same number of lizards, snakes, and chameleons. How many snakes are there at the zoo?

_____

2. The Smithfield Zoo buys 3 times as much birdseed as the Parker Zoo. If the Smithfield Zoo buys 2,553 pounds of birdseed, how many pounds of birdseed does the Parker Zoo buy?

_____

3. A zookeeper feeds the penguins 249 pounds of food over a period of 3 months. If he feeds the penguins the same amount of food each month, how many pounds of food does he feed them per month?

_____

4. In January, 233 people visited the zoo. In February, 148 people visited, and 249 came in March. What was the average number of people who visited the zoo each month?

_____

2-Digit By 2-Digit Division

Solve each problem.

Example:

$17\overline{)68}$ **Think:** What number times 17 is closest to 68? (Round to guess.)

$20 \times$ **?** $= 70$
$20 \times$ **3** $= 60$
$17 \times$ **3** $= 51$

Try 3:

$$\begin{array}{r} 3 \\ 17\overline{)68} \\ -51 \\ \hline \mathbf{17} \end{array}$$

Think: My remainder should always be less than my divisor, so I need to add to my quotient.

Try 4:

$$\begin{array}{r} \mathbf{4} \\ 17\overline{)68} \\ -68 \\ \hline 0 \end{array}$$

1. $15\overline{)42}$

2. $23\overline{)47}$

3. $47\overline{)53}$

4. $25\overline{)60}$

5. $11\overline{)22}$

6. $12\overline{)20}$

7. $17\overline{)27}$

8. $13\overline{)14}$

9. $14\overline{)52}$

10. $12\overline{)48}$

11. $12\overline{)13}$

12. $17\overline{)25}$

3-Digit by 2-Digit Division with Remainders

Solve each problem.

Example:

$$\begin{array}{r} 1 \\ 45\overline{)581} \end{array} \qquad \begin{array}{r} 12 \\ 45\overline{)581} \\ -45\downarrow \\ \hline 131 \end{array} \qquad \begin{array}{r} 12 \\ 45\overline{)581} \\ -45 \\ \hline 131 \\ -90 \\ \hline 41 \end{array} \qquad \begin{array}{r} \textbf{12 R41} \\ 45\overline{)581} \\ -45 \\ \hline 131 \\ -90 \\ \hline 41 \end{array}$$

↑ dividend

⌞ These should be equal. ⟶

Check: Multiply the quotient by the divisor. Add the remainder.

$$\begin{array}{r} 45 \leftarrow \text{quotient} \\ \times\ 12 \leftarrow \text{divisor} \\ \hline 90 \\ +\ 450 \\ \hline 540 \\ +\ 41 \leftarrow \text{remainder} \\ \hline \textbf{581} \leftarrow \text{dividend} \end{array}$$

1. $46\overline{)441}$

2. $20\overline{)635}$

3. $74\overline{)318}$

4. $22\overline{)415}$

5. $37\overline{)862}$

6. $81\overline{)569}$

7. $77\overline{)138}$

8. $99\overline{)775}$

9. $56\overline{)875}$

10. $49\overline{)995}$

11. $18\overline{)296}$

12. $17\overline{)607}$

4-Digit by 2-Digit Division with Remainders

Solve each problem.

Example:

$$72\overline{)8,724}$$

$$\begin{array}{r} 1 \\ 72\overline{)8,724} \\ -72\downarrow \\ \hline 152 \end{array}$$

$$\begin{array}{r} 12 \\ 72\overline{)8,724} \\ -72 \\ \hline 152 \\ -144\downarrow \\ \hline 84 \end{array}$$

$$\begin{array}{r} 121 \\ 72\overline{)8,724} \\ -72 \\ \hline 152 \\ -144 \\ \hline 84 \\ -72 \\ \hline 12 \end{array}$$

$$\begin{array}{r} \textbf{121 R12} \\ 72\overline{)8,724} \\ -72 \\ \hline 152 \\ -144 \\ \hline 84 \\ -72 \\ \hline 12 \end{array}$$

1. $92\overline{)1,274}$

2. $54\overline{)2,809}$

3. $98\overline{)9,108}$

4. $85\overline{)3,950}$

5. $93\overline{)7,728}$

6. $87\overline{)6,014}$

7. $76\overline{)6,975}$

8. $32\overline{)2,544}$

9. $74\overline{)4,096}$

Dividing Large Numbers: Problem Solving

Solve each problem.

1. Tyree's dad told him that his dog, Sparky, is 91 years old in dog years. If 1 human year is equal to 7 dog years, how many human years has Sparky been alive?

_____

2. Kimberly has had her cat for 198 months. About how many years is this? What is the remainder?

_____

3. George found out that 1 human year is about 25 rat years. Jason claims that his rat must be 208 in rat years! How many human years old would Jason's rat be in order for his claim to be correct? What is the remainder?

_____

4. Jeremy has started planning a birthday party for his younger brother David. David is 847 days old. How many weeks old is David?

_____

Division Review

Solve each problem.

1. $3\overline{)72}$ 2. $8\overline{)44}$ 3. $6\overline{)472}$ 4. $3\overline{)852}$

5. $4\overline{)2,408}$ 6. $2\overline{)1,240}$ 7. $16\overline{)67}$ 8. $10\overline{)6,473}$

9. $34\overline{)120}$ 10. $82\overline{)783}$ 11. $92\overline{)3,457}$ 12. $41\overline{)9,056}$

13. Natalie collects glass beads. She keeps the beads in small containers that hold 14 beads each. If she has 1,946 beads, how many containers does she have?

_____

14. Sam and John collected 2,248 baseball cards. If they put the cards in groups of 8, how many groups will they have?

_____

Multiplying Decimals: Placing Decimal Points

Solve each problem.

To multiply decimals, first multiply as you would with whole numbers. Then, count the total number of decimal places to the right of the decimal point in both factors. That is the number of decimal places in the product.

1.3×0.3

1.3	**1** decimal place
× 0.3	+ **1** decimal place
0.39	**2** decimal places

2.43×2.1

2.**43**	**2** decimal places
× 2.1	+ **1** decimal place
243	
+ 4860	
5.103	**3** decimal places

1.   0.5
    × 0.4

2.   0.7
    × 0.5

3.   0.55
    × 0.5

4.   3.9
    × 5.1

5.   7.3
    × 0.6

6.   0.7
    × 0.21

7.   0.7
    × 0.3

8.   0.12
    × 0.33

9.   45.3
    × 2.1

10.   0.62
    × 0.9

11.   0.637
    × 0.9

12.   0.35
    × 0.75

Multiplying Decimals by Powers of 10

Find each product. Use mental math.

To multiply by 10, move the decimal point **one** place to the right.	To multiply by 100, move the decimal point **two** places to the right. Add zeros for place holders.	To multiply by 1,000, move the decimal point **three** places to the right.
0.4 $$10 \times 0.4 = \mathbf{4}$$	**0.40** $$100 \times 0.40 = \mathbf{40}$$	**0.400** $$1{,}000 \times 0.400 = \mathbf{400}$$

1. $10 \times 0.06 =$

2. $100 \times 0.06 =$

3. $1{,}000 \times 0.06 =$

4. $10 \times 4.3 =$

5. $100 \times 4.3 =$

6. $1{,}000 \times 4.3 =$

7. $0.653 \times 1{,}000 =$

8. $1.09 \times 10 =$

9. $21.3 \times 10 =$

10. $1{,}000 \times 0.046 =$

11. $0.46 \times 1{,}000 =$

12. $0.0045 \times 10 =$

13. $100 \times 0.03 =$

Multiplying Decimals by 1-Digit Whole Numbers

Solve each problem.

Example: 32 × 0.43

Multiply the factors as if the decimal point is not there.

$$
\begin{array}{r}
0.43 \\
\times \quad 3 \\
\hline
129
\end{array}
$$

Count the total number of decimal places to the right of the decimal point in both factors. That is the number of decimal places in the product.

$$
\begin{array}{rl}
0.43 & \textbf{2 decimal places} \\
\times \quad 3 & + \textbf{0 decimal places} \\
\hline
\textbf{1.29} & \textbf{2 decimal places}
\end{array}
$$

1.
$$
\begin{array}{r}
0.4 \\
\times \ 6 \\
\hline
\end{array}
$$

2.
$$
\begin{array}{r}
0.9 \\
\times \ 3 \\
\hline
\end{array}
$$

3.
$$
\begin{array}{r}
0.12 \\
\times \ \ 7 \\
\hline
\end{array}
$$

4.
$$
\begin{array}{r}
4.9 \\
\times \ 8 \\
\hline
\end{array}
$$

5.
$$
\begin{array}{r}
4.5 \\
\times \ 3 \\
\hline
\end{array}
$$

6.
$$
\begin{array}{r}
2.81 \\
\times \ \ 4 \\
\hline
\end{array}
$$

7.
$$
\begin{array}{r}
1.76 \\
\times \ \ 5 \\
\hline
\end{array}
$$

8.
$$
\begin{array}{r}
3.03 \\
\times \ \ 6 \\
\hline
\end{array}
$$

9.
$$
\begin{array}{r}
2.8 \\
\times \ 4 \\
\hline
\end{array}
$$

10.
$$
\begin{array}{r}
6.2 \\
\times \ 3 \\
\hline
\end{array}
$$

11.
$$
\begin{array}{r}
3.7 \\
\times \ 5 \\
\hline
\end{array}
$$

12.
$$
\begin{array}{r}
0.17 \\
\times \ \ 4 \\
\hline
\end{array}
$$

Multiplying Money

Multiply. Remember to include the dollar sign and the decimal point.

To multiply money, follow these steps:

1. Multiply the top number by the bottom number. Regroup if necessary.

2. Count the number of places after the decimal point. When multiplying money, there are two places after the decimal point. Write a decimal point in the product two places from the right.

3. Write the dollar sign.

Example:

$$\begin{array}{r} \$5.00 \\ \times \quad 8 \\ \hline \$40.00 \end{array}$$

1.
$$\begin{array}{r} \$7.00 \\ \times \quad 5 \\ \hline \end{array}$$

2.
$$\begin{array}{r} \$4.00 \\ \times \quad 8 \\ \hline \end{array}$$

3.
$$\begin{array}{r} \$8.00 \\ \times \quad 3 \\ \hline \end{array}$$

4.
$$\begin{array}{r} \$9.00 \\ \times \quad 2 \\ \hline \end{array}$$

5.
$$\begin{array}{r} \$1.00 \\ \times \quad 4 \\ \hline \end{array}$$

6.
$$\begin{array}{r} \$3.00 \\ \times \quad 6 \\ \hline \end{array}$$

7.
$$\begin{array}{r} \$1.00 \\ \times \quad 7 \\ \hline \end{array}$$

8.
$$\begin{array}{r} \$7.00 \\ \times \quad 9 \\ \hline \end{array}$$

9.
$$\begin{array}{r} \$4.00 \\ \times \quad 6 \\ \hline \end{array}$$

10.
$$\begin{array}{r} \$6.00 \\ \times \quad 8 \\ \hline \end{array}$$

11.
$$\begin{array}{r} \$3.00 \\ \times \quad 3 \\ \hline \end{array}$$

12.
$$\begin{array}{r} \$4.00 \\ \times \quad 4 \\ \hline \end{array}$$

Multiplying Decimals

Multiply.

Multiply **1.4 × 0.2**

$$
\begin{array}{r}
1.4 \\
\times\ 0.2 \\
\hline
0.28
\end{array}
\qquad
\begin{array}{l}
\textbf{1}\ \text{decimal place} \\
+\ \textbf{1}\ \text{decimal place} \\
\hline
\textbf{2}\ \text{decimal places}
\end{array}
$$

1. $\begin{array}{r} 0.7 \\ \times\ 0.4 \\ \hline \end{array}$

2. $\begin{array}{r} 0.3 \\ \times\ 0.5 \\ \hline \end{array}$

3. $\begin{array}{r} 0.54 \\ \times\ 0.6 \\ \hline \end{array}$

4. $\begin{array}{r} 2.9 \\ \times\ 5.4 \\ \hline \end{array}$

5. $\begin{array}{r} 8.4 \\ \times\ 0.6 \\ \hline \end{array}$

6. $\begin{array}{r} 0.7 \\ \times\ 0.12 \\ \hline \end{array}$

7. $\begin{array}{r} 0.9 \\ \times\ 0.2 \\ \hline \end{array}$

8. $\begin{array}{r} 0.12 \\ \times\ 0.22 \\ \hline \end{array}$

9. $\begin{array}{r} 56.1 \\ \times\ 2.1 \\ \hline \end{array}$

10. $\begin{array}{r} 0.45 \\ \times\ 0.9 \\ \hline \end{array}$

11. $\begin{array}{r} 0.724 \\ \times\ 0.6 \\ \hline \end{array}$

12. $\begin{array}{r} 0.46 \\ \times\ 0.87 \\ \hline \end{array}$

13. $\begin{array}{r} 4.95 \\ \times\ 0.3 \\ \hline \end{array}$

14. $\begin{array}{r} 0.2 \\ \times\ 7.8 \\ \hline \end{array}$

15. $\begin{array}{r} 9.12 \\ \times\ 4.3 \\ \hline \end{array}$

16. $\begin{array}{r} 65.1 \\ \times\ 0.25 \\ \hline \end{array}$

Multiplying Decimals with Zeros in the Products

Solve each problem.

Sometimes, more decimal places are needed than there are digits in the answer. In this case, add zeros for the additional digits.

Example: 1.05 × 0.03

Multiply as you would with whole numbers.

$$
\begin{array}{r}
{\scriptstyle 1} \\
1.05 \\
\times\ 0.03 \\
\hline
315
\end{array}
$$

Count the total number of decimal places. Then, place the decimal point in the answer. Write zeros to fill the extra places.

$$
\begin{array}{rl}
1.\mathbf{05} & \textbf{2 decimal places} \\
\times\ 0.\mathbf{03} & \underline{+\ \textbf{2 decimal places}} \\
\mathbf{0.0315} & \textbf{4 decimal places needed in} \\
\uparrow & \text{answer but only 3 numbers.}
\end{array}
$$

Add zero as a placeholder.

1.
$$
\begin{array}{r}
0.091 \\
\times\ 0.02 \\
\hline
\end{array}
$$

2.
$$
\begin{array}{r}
0.0072 \\
\times\ \ 0.07 \\
\hline
\end{array}
$$

3.
$$
\begin{array}{r}
0.0043 \\
\times\ \ \ 0.9 \\
\hline
\end{array}
$$

4.
$$
\begin{array}{r}
0.0053 \\
\times\ \ 0.33 \\
\hline
\end{array}
$$

5.
$$
\begin{array}{r}
0.305 \\
\times\ 0.008 \\
\hline
\end{array}
$$

6.
$$
\begin{array}{r}
0.165 \\
\times\ 0.08 \\
\hline
\end{array}
$$

7.
$$
\begin{array}{r}
0.002 \\
\times\ \ 9.7 \\
\hline
\end{array}
$$

8.
$$
\begin{array}{r}
0.0047 \\
\times\ \ 0.83 \\
\hline
\end{array}
$$

9.
$$
\begin{array}{r}
0.309 \\
\times\ 0.09 \\
\hline
\end{array}
$$

Multiplying Decimals: Word Problems

Use the information to solve each problem.

Michael is in college studying to become a nurse. In many of his laboratory classes, he must measure quantities and record data.

1. Michael performed blood tests using 5 test tubes. Each tube contained 12.73 milliliters of blood. How much blood did he test in all?

2. Michael's lab partner was using a mixture of water and iodine in 8 beakers. Each beaker held 7.012 milliliters of the mixture. How much of the mixture did he have altogether?

3. Michael wrapped a cloth bandage around a patient's arm. He wrapped the bandage 15 times before securing it. He used 9.12 centimeters each time he wrapped the bandage. How long was the bandage that he used?

4. In chemistry class, Michael took a package of salt and split the contents evenly into 9 groups. Each group weighed 0.07 kilograms. How much salt was in the original package?

Multiplying Decimals Review

Solve each problem.

1. 0.07
   × 18

2. 0.7
   × 0.6

3. 0.258
   × 0.4

4. 3.14
   × 0.86

5. 0.07
   × 0.9

6. 0.075
   × 0.4

7. 2.87
   × 0.05

8. 0.003
   × 9.26

9. 0.27
   × 0.9

10. 2.54
    × 0.7

11. 8.3
    × 9.2

12. 0.062
    × 0.03

13. A machine part weighs 1.34 ounces. How much do 50 of the same part weigh?

14. In the turtle trot race, a turtle travels at a rate of 0.09 miles per hour. How far will the turtle travel in 0.40 hours?

Dividing Decimals:
Adding Zeros to the Dividend

Divide. Check your work.

Step 1	**Step 2**	**Step 3**
Divide the tenths.	Write a 0 in the hundredths place.	Write another 0 in the thousandths place. Bring down and divide.

Step 1

$$
\begin{array}{r}
0.6 \\
4\overline{)2.5} \\
-24 \\
\hline
1
\end{array}
$$

Step 2

$$
\begin{array}{r}
0.62 \\
4\overline{)2.50} \\
-24 \\
\hline
10 \\
-8 \\
\hline
2
\end{array}
$$

←Write a zero here.
←Write a zero here.
Divide by 4.

Step 3

$$
\begin{array}{r}
0.625 \\
4\overline{)2.500} \\
-24 \\
\hline
10 \\
-8 \\
\hline
20 \\
-20 \\
\hline
0
\end{array}
$$

1. $5\overline{)2.7}$ 2. $4\overline{)4.6}$ 3. $6\overline{)5.7}$ 4. $4\overline{)0.31}$

5. $5\overline{)8.1}$ 6. $4\overline{)6.3}$ 7. $5\overline{)4.19}$ 8. $5\overline{)3.74}$

9. $4\overline{)53.4}$ 10. $18\overline{)9.63}$ 11. $40\overline{)53.6}$ 12. $16\overline{)5.2}$

Dividing Decimals by Powers of 10

Try some on your own. Underline the basic fact, and circle the zeros to add on.

> You can use basic facts and patterns to help you divide decimals by powers of 10.
>
> **Examples:**
> $$0.5 \div 10 = \textbf{0.05}$$
> $$0.5 \div 100 = \textbf{0.005}$$
> $$0.5 \div 1,000 = \textbf{0.0005}$$

1. $6.2 \div 10 = $ _____

    $6.2 \div 100 = $ _____

    $6.2 \div 1,000 = $ _____

2. $525.3 \div 10 = $ _____

    $525.3 \div 100 = $ _____

    $525.3 \div 1,000 = $ _____

3. $1,050.9 \div 10 = $ _____

    $1,050.9 \div 100 = $ _____

    $1,050.9 \div 1,000 = $ _____

4. $90.565 \div 10 = $ _____

    $90.565 \div 100 = $ _____

    $90.565 \div 1,000 = $ _____

Dividing a Decimal by a Whole Number

Solve each problem.

Example: 3.25 ÷ 5

Place the decimal point in the quotient directly above the decimal point in the dividend.	Divide as you would for whole numbers.	Check by multiplying.
5)3.25 **Remember:** The dividend is the number that will be divided.	$$\begin{array}{r} 0.65 \\ 5\overline{)3.25} \\ -3\,0 \\ \hline 25 \\ -25 \\ \hline 0 \end{array}$$	$$\begin{array}{r} 0.65 \\ \times\quad 5 \\ \hline 3.25 \end{array}$$

1. 8)2.4

2. 8)0.24

3. 3)0.69

4. 3)0.069

5. 2)45.4

6. 2)4.54

7. 7)34.37

8. 5)0.105

9. 6)120.6

Dividing a Decimal by a Decimal

Solve each problem.

To divide by a decimal, you must move the decimal point to make the divisor a whole number.

Example: 5.44 ÷ 1.6

Move the decimal point one place to the right to make the divisor a whole number. Move the decimal point in the dividend the same number of places.

Divide as you would with whole numbers.

$$
\begin{array}{r}
3.4 \\
16\overline{)54.4} \\
-48 \\
\hline
64 \\
-64 \\
\hline
0
\end{array}
$$

$$1.6\overline{)5.44} \longrightarrow 16\overline{)54.4}$$

1. $0.6\overline{)5.4}$

2. $0.9\overline{)0.18}$

3. $1.4\overline{)13.86}$

4. $0.86\overline{)0.688}$

5. $1.7\overline{)10.54}$

6. $2.4\overline{)16.8}$

7. $0.07\overline{)0.035}$

8. $0.92\overline{)0.736}$

9. $0.005\overline{)0.015}$

Dividing Decimals: Word Problems

Solve each problem.

When finding a unit cost, divide the total cost by the number of units. **Total Cost ÷ Number of Units = Unit Cost**

Maria bought a 15-ounce bag of tortilla chips for $2.25. What is the cost per ounce?

$$
\begin{array}{r}
\$0.15 \\
15\overline{)\$2.25} \\
-15 \\
\hline
75 \\
-75 \\
\hline
0
\end{array}
$$

← Unit Cost (per ounce)
← Total Cost

Number of Units

1. At Orchard Street Market, 4.5 pounds of pears cost $2.97. What is the cost per pound?

_____

2. Mrs. Parks bought 30 ice cream bars for her daughter's class party. She paid $12.60. How much did each ice cream bar cost?

_____

3. Sandra bought a 32.5-ounce package of mixed nuts for $7.15. What was the cost per ounce?

_____

4. A $2.56 can of lemonade mix will make 64 cups of lemonade. What is the cost per cup?

_____

Dividing Decimals Review

Solve each problem.

1. $8\overline{)7.2}$ 2. $18\overline{)7.56}$ 3. $6\overline{)1.38}$ 4. $35\overline{)74.9}$

5. $4\overline{)32.12}$ 6. $14\overline{)70.98}$ 7. $36\overline{)0.324}$ 8. $58\overline{)0.3654}$

9. $0.6\overline{)0.048}$ 10. $0.56\overline{)1.288}$

11. $0.8\overline{)184}$ 12. $0.25\overline{)9}$

13. An 11-ounce bottle of shampoo costs $2.97. What is the cost per ounce?

_____

14. A 12-story building is 127.2 feet tall. How tall is each story if they are all the same height?

_____

Writing Improper Fractions as Mixed or Whole Numbers

Write each improper fraction as a mixed or whole number.

Example:

$\frac{14}{3}$ can be rewritten as $14 \div 3$ or $3\overline{)14}$.

$\frac{14}{3}$ is an improper fraction.

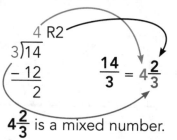

$\frac{14}{3} = 4\frac{2}{3}$

$4\frac{2}{3}$ is a mixed number.

The **4** becomes the whole number. The **2** becomes the numerator of the fraction; the denominator is still **3**.

1. $\frac{15}{2} =$

2. $\frac{7}{4} =$

3. $\frac{20}{7} =$

4. $\frac{43}{5} =$

5. $\frac{23}{8} =$

6. $\frac{21}{5} =$

7. $\frac{31}{12} =$

8. $\frac{5}{2} =$

9. $\frac{13}{8} =$

10. $\frac{11}{4} =$

11. $\frac{49}{9} =$

12. $\frac{41}{6} =$

13. $\frac{23}{3} =$

14. $\frac{45}{4} =$

15. $\frac{60}{5} =$

16. $\frac{23}{7} =$

17. $\frac{72}{6} =$

18. $\frac{16}{2} =$

Writing Mixed Numbers as Improper Fractions

Write each mixed number as an improper fraction.

To change a mixed number to an improper fraction:	**Examples:**
1. Multiply the denominator by the whole number.	$3\frac{1}{3} = \frac{(3 \times 3) + 1}{3}$ $\qquad$ $4\frac{5}{8} = \frac{(8 \times 4) + 5}{8}$
2. Add the numerator.	$= \frac{9 + 1}{3}$ $\qquad\qquad$ $= \frac{32 + 5}{8}$
3. Keep the denominator.	$= \frac{10}{3}$ $\qquad\qquad$ $= \frac{37}{8}$

1. $2\frac{1}{3} =$ $\qquad$ 2. $6\frac{3}{4} =$ $\qquad$ 3. $1\frac{1}{12} =$ $\qquad$ 4. $3\frac{1}{8} =$

5. $7\frac{3}{5} =$ $\qquad$ 6. $1\frac{9}{10} =$ $\qquad$ 7. $3\frac{2}{5} =$ $\qquad$ 8. $9\frac{4}{11} =$

9. $3\frac{6}{7} =$ $\qquad$ 10. $5\frac{4}{5} =$ $\qquad$ 11. $4\frac{5}{12} =$ $\qquad$ 12. $6\frac{7}{11} =$

Simplifying Fractions

Write each fraction in simplest form.

A fraction is simplified when 1 is the only number that divides into *both* the numerator and the denominator.

To simplify, you must divide the numerator and denominator by the same number.

Examples:

$$\frac{4}{8} = \frac{4 \div 4}{8 \div 4}$$

$$= \frac{1}{2}$$

$$\frac{12}{18} = \frac{12 \div 2}{18 \div 2}$$

$$= \frac{6}{9}$$

$\frac{6}{9}$ is not simplified.

$$\frac{6}{9} = \frac{6 \div 3}{9 \div 3}$$

$$= \frac{2}{3}$$

1. $\frac{2}{8} =$

2. $\frac{6}{15} =$

3. $\frac{8}{24} =$

4. $\frac{4}{6} =$

5. $\frac{5}{15} =$

6. $\frac{6}{10} =$

7. $\frac{6}{8} =$

8. $\frac{2}{24} =$

9. $\frac{8}{12} =$

10. $\frac{3}{9} =$

11. $\frac{6}{24} =$

12. $\frac{10}{12} =$

13. $\frac{6}{12} =$

14. $\frac{5}{20} =$

15. $\frac{14}{14} =$

Multiplying Fractions

Use the grids to solve each problem.

$\frac{1}{2} \times \frac{1}{4}$ can be visualized as:

$\frac{1}{2} \times \frac{1}{4} = \frac{1}{8}$

$\frac{2}{3} \times \frac{4}{5}$ can be visualized as:

$\frac{2}{3} \times \frac{4}{5} = \frac{8}{15}$

1.
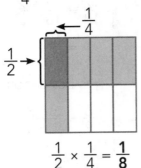

$\frac{1}{3} \times \frac{2}{5} = $ _____

2.

$\frac{1}{4} \times \frac{1}{3} = $ _____

3.
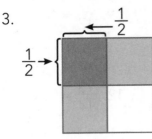

$\frac{1}{2} \times \frac{1}{2} = $ _____

4.

$\frac{3}{4} \times \frac{1}{2} = $ _____

Multiplying Fractions by Whole Numbers

Solve each problem. Simplify if possible.

When multiplying a whole number and a fraction:

1. Rewrite the whole number as a fraction. (Write a denominator of 1.)

2. Multiply the numerators.

3. Multiply the denominators.

4. Simplify if possible.

Examples:

$$8 \times \frac{3}{8} = \frac{8}{1} \times \frac{3}{8}$$

$$= \frac{8 \times 3}{1 \times 8}$$

$$= \frac{24}{8}$$

$$= 3$$

$$\frac{3}{4} \times 6 = \frac{3}{4} \times \frac{6}{1}$$

$$= \frac{3 \times 6}{4 \times 1}$$

$$= \frac{18}{5}$$

$$= 4\frac{2}{4} = 4\frac{1}{2}$$

1. $3 \times \frac{2}{3} =$

2. $\frac{4}{5} \times 2 =$

3. $1 \times \frac{6}{7} =$

4. $2 \times \frac{4}{7} =$

5. $\frac{2}{5} \times 6 =$

6. $3 \times \frac{3}{10} =$

7. $9 \times \frac{3}{4} =$

8. $6 \times \frac{3}{10} =$

9. $8 \times \frac{1}{6} =$

10. $2 \times \frac{6}{7} =$

11. $6 \times \frac{1}{10} =$

12. $\frac{3}{8} \times 4 =$

Multiplying Fractions by Mixed Numbers

Solve each problem. Simplify if possible.

When multiplying a mixed number and a fraction:

1. Rewrite the mixed number as an improper fraction.
2. Multiply the numerators.
3. Multiply the denominators.
4. Simplify if possible.

Examples:

$$2\frac{1}{3} \times \frac{4}{5} = \frac{7}{3} \times \frac{4}{5}$$
$$= \frac{7 \times 4}{3 \times 5}$$
$$= \frac{28}{15}$$
$$= 1\frac{13}{15}$$

$$\frac{1}{3} \times 2\frac{2}{3} = \frac{1}{3} \times \frac{8}{3}$$
$$= \frac{1 \times 8}{3 \times 3}$$
$$= \frac{8}{9}$$
$$= \frac{8}{9}$$

1. $\frac{1}{2} \times 1\frac{1}{8} =$

2. $2\frac{1}{3} \times \frac{1}{3} =$

3. $4\frac{1}{2} \times \frac{1}{3} =$

4. $2\frac{2}{3} \times \frac{3}{7} =$

5. $3\frac{1}{2} \times \frac{1}{4} =$

6. $\frac{3}{5} \times 3\frac{1}{2} =$

7. $\frac{2}{5} \times 3\frac{1}{3} =$

8. $\frac{2}{3} \times 5\frac{1}{4} =$

9. $4\frac{3}{4} \times \frac{1}{3} =$

10. $\frac{1}{9} \times 2\frac{1}{2} =$

11. $\frac{1}{2} \times 1\frac{3}{5} =$

12. $\frac{1}{6} \times 3\frac{1}{3} =$

13. $4\frac{2}{3} \times \frac{3}{4} =$

14. $9\frac{1}{2} \times \frac{1}{6} =$

15. $3\frac{3}{4} \times \frac{5}{12} =$

Multiplying Whole Numbers by Mixed Numbers

Solve each problem. Simplify if possible.

When multiplying a mixed number and a whole number:

1. Rewrite the numbers as improper fractions.
2. Multiply the numerators.
3. Multiply the denominators.
4. Simplify if possible.

Examples:

$$2\frac{1}{3} \times 4 = \frac{7}{3} \times \frac{4}{1}$$
$$= \frac{7 \times 4}{3 \times 1}$$
$$= \frac{28}{3}$$
$$= 9\frac{1}{3}$$

$$6 \times 3\frac{2}{3} = \frac{6}{1} \times \frac{11}{3}$$
$$= \frac{6 \times 11}{1 \times 3}$$
$$= \frac{66}{3}$$
$$= 22$$

1. $3\frac{1}{4} \times 2 =$

2. $1\frac{4}{5} \times 2 =$

3. $1 \times 3\frac{6}{7} =$

4. $2 \times 4\frac{4}{7} =$

5. $3\frac{2}{5} \times 2 =$

6. $3 \times 2\frac{3}{10} =$

7. $9 \times 1\frac{3}{4} =$

8. $3 \times 4\frac{3}{10} =$

9. $3 \times 4\frac{1}{6} =$

10. $2 \times 3\frac{6}{7} =$

11. $6 \times 2\frac{1}{10} =$

12. $5\frac{3}{8} \times 4 =$

13. $2\frac{3}{10} \times 4 =$

14. $5 \times 2\frac{5}{9} =$

15. $5\frac{1}{7} \times 2 =$

Multiplying Mixed Numbers

Solve each problem. Simplify if possible.

When multiplying mixed numbers:

1. Rewrite the numbers as improper fractions.
2. Multiply the numerators.
3. Multiply the denominators.
4. Simplify if possible.

Examples:

$$2\frac{1}{4} \times 1\frac{1}{2} = \frac{9}{4} \times \frac{3}{2}$$
$$= \frac{9 \times 3}{4 \times 2}$$
$$= \frac{27}{8}$$
$$= 3\frac{3}{8}$$

$$1\frac{1}{3} \times 2\frac{1}{8} = \frac{4}{3} \times \frac{17}{8}$$
$$= \frac{4 \times 17}{3 \times 8}$$
$$= \frac{68}{24}$$
$$= 2\frac{20}{24} = 2\frac{5}{6}$$

1. $3\frac{3}{4} \times 2\frac{2}{3} =$

2. $1\frac{1}{4} \times 2\frac{1}{2} =$

3. $2\frac{1}{5} \times 2\frac{1}{4} =$

4. $1\frac{1}{5} \times 2\frac{1}{6} =$

5. $1\frac{3}{5} \times 1\frac{2}{5} =$

6. $2\frac{1}{2} \times 3\frac{1}{3} =$

7. $4\frac{1}{2} \times 1\frac{2}{3} =$

8. $2\frac{4}{5} \times 5\frac{1}{4} =$

9. $2\frac{3}{8} \times 2\frac{1}{3} =$

Multiplying Fractions: Problem Solving

Solve each problem. Simplify if possible.

1. Austin wanted to go to the movie theater. It is $3\frac{3}{5}$ miles from his house. Austin decided to take his motor scooter, but it broke down $\frac{2}{3}$ of the way there. How far was Austin from his house?

2. Austin purchased $\frac{2}{3}$ of a pound of yum-yum treats. If yum-yum treats are $6.00 per pound, how much did Austin pay?

3. At the theater, Austin met his friends, who had purchased 1 large popcorn. Only $\frac{3}{4}$ of it was left. Austin ate $\frac{1}{3}$ of what was left. How much of the popcorn did Austin eat?

4. Each night, Austin goes to bed and sleeps for an average of $8\frac{2}{3}$ hours. In one week, how many hours of sleep does Austin get?

Multiplying Fractions Review

Solve each problem. Simplify if possible.

1. $\dfrac{1}{4} \times \dfrac{5}{6} =$

2. $\dfrac{7}{10} \times \dfrac{1}{3} =$

3. $\dfrac{3}{7} \times \dfrac{1}{6} =$

4. $\dfrac{9}{10} \times \dfrac{5}{15} =$

5. $8 \times \dfrac{3}{4} =$

6. $4 \times \dfrac{5}{12} =$

7. $\dfrac{2}{3} \times 2\dfrac{4}{7} =$

8. $3\dfrac{1}{8} \times \dfrac{2}{3} =$

9. $\dfrac{5}{6} \times 2\dfrac{1}{4} =$

10. $1 \times 3\dfrac{2}{3} =$

11. $5 \times 1\dfrac{1}{4} =$

12. $6 \times 2\dfrac{3}{4} =$

13. For 16 days, Zoe practiced the piano for $\dfrac{3}{4}$ of an hour each day. What is the total time that Zoe spent practicing the piano?

14. Jake rides his bicycle $\dfrac{1}{4}$ mile to and from school for 6 days in the month of September. How many miles did Jake ride his bicycle in September?

Reciprocals

Write the reciprocal of each number or fraction.

Reciprocals are numbers that, when multiplied, have a product of 1. To divide fractions, you must first find the reciprocal of the divisor.

Examples: $\dfrac{7}{4}$

To write the reciprocal of $\dfrac{7}{4}$, reverse the numerator and the denominator.

$$\dfrac{7}{4} \diagup\!\!\!\!\diagdown \dfrac{4}{7}$$

To check your answer, multiply the original number by its reciprocal. If the product is 1, the reciprocal is correct.

$$\dfrac{7}{4} \times \dfrac{4}{7} = \dfrac{28}{28} = 1$$

$4\dfrac{1}{3}$

$$4\dfrac{1}{3} = \dfrac{13}{3}$$

$$\dfrac{13}{3} \diagup\!\!\!\!\diagdown \dfrac{3}{13}$$

$$4\dfrac{1}{3} = \dfrac{13}{3} \times \dfrac{3}{13} = \dfrac{39}{39} = 1$$

1. $\dfrac{11}{5} \times \boxed{\dfrac{\ }{\ }} = 1$

2. $2\dfrac{1}{4} \times \boxed{\dfrac{\ }{\ }} = 1$

3. $9 \times \boxed{\dfrac{\ }{\ }} = 1$

4. $\dfrac{3}{10} \times \boxed{\dfrac{\ }{\ }} = 1$

5. $\dfrac{1}{7} \times \boxed{\dfrac{\ }{\ }} = 1$

6. $4\dfrac{5}{8} \times \boxed{\dfrac{\ }{\ }} = 1$

7. $\dfrac{15}{11} \times \boxed{\dfrac{\ }{\ }} = 1$

8. $\dfrac{1}{6} \times \boxed{\dfrac{\ }{\ }} = 1$

9. $\dfrac{3}{4} \times \boxed{\dfrac{\ }{\ }} = 1$

Dividing Fractions and Whole Numbers

Solve each problem. Simplify if possible.

Dividing a fraction by a whole number:

$$\frac{4}{5} \div 8$$

Write the whole number as a fraction with a denominator of 1.

$$\frac{4}{5} \div 8 = \frac{4}{5} \div \frac{8}{1}$$

Multiply the dividend by the reciprocal of the divisor. Simplify if possible.

$$\frac{4}{5} \times \frac{1}{8} = \frac{4 \times 1}{5 \times 8} = \frac{4}{40} = \mathbf{\frac{1}{10}}$$

Dividing a whole number by a fraction:

$$5 \div \frac{3}{4}$$

Write the whole number as a fraction with a denominator of 1.

$$5 \div \frac{3}{4} = \frac{5}{1} \div \frac{3}{4}$$

Multiply the dividend by the reciprocal of the divisor. Simplify if possible.

$$\frac{5}{1} \times \frac{4}{3} = \frac{5 \times 4}{1 \times 3} = \frac{20}{3} = \mathbf{6\frac{2}{3}}$$

1. $6 \div \frac{4}{9} =$

2. $5 \div \frac{1}{7} =$

3. $\frac{4}{7} \div 8 =$

4. $4 \div \frac{3}{5} =$

5. $\frac{5}{8} \div 5 =$

6. $\frac{9}{10} \div 4 =$

7. $\frac{9}{4} \div 6 =$

8. $4 \div \frac{5}{3} =$

9. $\frac{4}{3} \div 5 =$

10. $\frac{10}{9} \div 4 =$

11. $\frac{7}{4} \div 3 =$

12. $8 \div \frac{2}{3} =$

Dividing Fractions

Solve each problem. Simplify if possible.

To divide by a fraction, multiply the dividend by the reciprocal of the divisor.

$$\text{dividend} \longrightarrow \frac{4}{5} \div \frac{3}{4} \longleftarrow \text{divisor}$$

The reciprocal of $\frac{3}{4}$ is $\frac{4}{3}$.

$$\frac{4}{5} \times \frac{4}{3} = \frac{4 \times 4}{5 \times 3} = \frac{16}{15} = 1\frac{1}{15}$$

1. $\frac{7}{2} \div \frac{1}{2} =$

2. $\frac{4}{3} \div \frac{2}{3} =$

3. $\frac{6}{4} \div \frac{3}{4} =$

4. $\frac{7}{8} \div \frac{3}{5} =$

5. $\frac{9}{2} \div \frac{1}{3} =$

6. $\frac{8}{3} \div \frac{2}{5} =$

7. $\frac{15}{4} \div \frac{3}{7} =$

8. $\frac{2}{3} \div \frac{3}{7} =$

9. $\frac{5}{6} \div \frac{5}{6} =$

10. $\frac{3}{8} \div \frac{3}{4} =$

11. $\frac{3}{4} \div \frac{5}{2} =$

12. $\frac{4}{5} \div \frac{4}{3} =$

13. $\frac{5}{8} \div \frac{1}{8} =$

14. $\frac{4}{7} \div \frac{2}{7} =$

15. $\frac{5}{8} \div \frac{3}{4} =$

16. $\frac{2}{5} \div \frac{4}{6} =$

Dividing Mixed Numbers

Divide. Write each quotient in simplest form.

To divide mixed numbers, first write each mixed number as a fraction.

$$3\frac{4}{5} \div 2\frac{3}{4} = \frac{19}{5} \div \frac{11}{4}$$

$$= \frac{19}{5} \times \frac{4}{11}$$

$$= \frac{19 \times 4}{5 \times 11}$$

$$= \frac{76}{55}$$

$$= 1\frac{21}{55}$$

Write each mixed number as an improper fraction.

Multiply the first fraction by the reciprocal of the second.

1. $9\frac{1}{2} \div 1\frac{7}{8} =$

2. $2\frac{1}{2} \div 3 =$

3. $3\frac{3}{4} \div 2\frac{3}{8} =$

4. $2\frac{3}{4} \div 4 =$

5. $2\frac{3}{4} \div 1\frac{3}{4} =$

6. $4\frac{2}{3} \div 2 =$

7. $6 \div 1\frac{1}{5} =$

8. $10\frac{1}{8} \div 1\frac{3}{4} =$

9. $3\frac{3}{5} \div 2\frac{1}{3} =$

10. $8 \div 2\frac{3}{8} =$

11. $12\frac{1}{2} \div 2\frac{1}{2} =$

12. $2\frac{1}{8} \div 2\frac{1}{2} =$

Dividing Mixed Numbers and Whole Numbers

Solve each problem. Simplify if possible.

Example: $3\frac{4}{5} \div 2$

Write each mixed number as an improper fraction. If the dividend or the divisor is a whole number, write it as a fraction with a denominator of 1.

$$3\frac{4}{5} \div 2 = \frac{19}{5} \div \frac{2}{1}$$

Multiply the dividend by the reciprocal of the divisor. Simplify if possible.

$$\frac{19}{5} \div \frac{2}{1} = \frac{19}{5} \times \frac{1}{2} = \frac{19 \times 1}{5 \times 2} = \frac{19}{10} = 1\frac{9}{10}$$

1. $11\frac{1}{2} \div 2\frac{7}{8} =$

2. $3\frac{1}{2} \div 2 =$

3. $4\frac{1}{4} \div 3\frac{1}{8} =$

4. $3\frac{3}{4} \div 5 =$

5. $3\frac{1}{2} \div 1\frac{3}{4} =$

6. $6\frac{1}{3} \div 2 =$

7. $8 \div 1\frac{1}{5} =$

8. $12\frac{3}{8} \div 2\frac{3}{4} =$

9. $5\frac{3}{5} \div 4\frac{2}{3} =$

10. $9 \div 2\frac{5}{8} =$

11. $7\frac{1}{2} \div 2\frac{1}{2} =$

12. $1\frac{1}{4} \div 2\frac{1}{2} =$

13. $7\frac{3}{12} \div 3\frac{1}{2} =$

14. $7 \div 2\frac{1}{3} =$

15. $4\frac{1}{6} \div 5 =$

Dividing Fractions: Problem Solving

Solve each problem. Simplify if possible.

1. A box contains 10 ounces of cereal. If one serving is $1\frac{1}{4}$ ounces, how many servings are in the box?

_____

2. A can contains $22\frac{3}{4}$ ounces of soup. If one can contains $3\frac{1}{2}$ servings of soup, how many ounces are in one serving?

_____

3. Ten melons weigh $17\frac{1}{2}$ pounds. What is the average weight of each melon?

_____

4. Chris bought $\frac{3}{4}$ of a pound of grapes to put in his lunches. If he eats the same amount each day and finishes the grapes in 5 days, how many pounds does he eat each day?

_____

Dividing Fractions Review

Write the reciprocal of each number, mixed number, or fraction.

1. $\frac{2}{3} =$ 2. $\frac{7}{4} =$ 3. $4\frac{1}{2} =$ 4. $5 =$ 5. $11\frac{1}{3} =$

Solve each problem. Simplify if possible.

6. $4 \div \frac{1}{6} =$

7. $3 \div \frac{1}{8} =$

8. $6 \div \frac{1}{5} =$

9. $5 \div \frac{5}{7} =$

10. $4 \div \frac{3}{5} =$

11. $\frac{3}{4} \div \frac{4}{5} =$

12. $\frac{2}{7} \div \frac{3}{5} =$

13. $2\frac{2}{3} \div \frac{3}{6} =$

14. $1\frac{3}{8} \div \frac{2}{4} =$

15. $\frac{3}{8} \div 3 =$

16. $\frac{3}{8} \div 2 =$

17. $3\frac{3}{5} \div 8 =$

Solve each problem. Simplify if possible.

18. Each bead on Josie's necklace is $\frac{3}{4}$ of an inch long. All of the beads together measure $3\frac{3}{4}$ inches. How many beads are part of her necklace?

_____

19. Keisha bought $\frac{1}{2}$ of a pound of cheese on Monday. For how many days can she eat $\frac{1}{8}$ of a pound of cheese?

_____

Prime and Composite Numbers

Use a factor tree to find the prime factors for each number. If the number is prime, write *prime* below the number.

A **prime number** is any whole number that has only two factors, itself and 1.

5 is a prime number. It has only two factors: 5 and 1.

Any number that is not a prime number is a **composite number**. **Prime factorization** is finding the prime factors of a number. A factor tree can be used to find the prime factors.

To find the prime factors of 24, start with any two factors that equal 24.

The prime factors of 24 are 3, 2, 2, and 2.

$24 = \mathbf{3 \times 2 \times 2 \times 2}$

1. 28

2. 21

3. 7

4. 48

Prime and Composite Numbers

Use a factor tree to find the prime factors for each number. If the number is prime, write *prime* below the number.

1. 36

2. 31

3. 32

4. 24

5. 67

6. 18

Prime and Composite Numbers

Use a factor tree to find the prime factors for each number. If the number is prime, write *prime* below the number.

1. 20

2. 50

3. 27

4. 11

5. 55

6. 42

Division Riddles

1. What is my quotient?

   My dividend is 63. I like to be divided by an odd number. My divisor is the answer to 14 ÷ 2. What is my quotient?

   _____

2. What is my divisor?

   My quotient is 424. But my dividend is twice as many. I am used a lot when problems ask for a half. My whole problem is full of even numbers, so what is my divisor?

   _____

3. What is my dividend?

   I am an odd, 2-digit number. If you add my divisor and my quotient together, you will get the numeral 14. You might even think my divisor and quotient are twins. If you add the 2 digits in my dividend, you will get 13. What is my dividend?

   _____

Just Above Average Division

Find the averages. Match each problem with its answer.

You find an average by dividing the **sum** of a group numbers by the number of **addends**. For example, to find the average of 2, 4, and 6, add 2 + 4 + 6 = 12. There are 3 numbers (2, 4, and 6), so divide 12 by 3, which equals 4. That's the average.

1. 21, 34, 44   A. 96

2. 278, 246   B. 67

3. 85, 100, 100, 100, 95   C. 190

4. 4, 6, 7, 12, 11   D. 33

5. 125, 248, 214, 173   E. 8

6. 81, 57, 63   F. 262

Face Puzzles — Part 1

Ms. Hansen is creating mystery picture puzzles of Graham, Libby, and Alicia. Solve the equation below each puzzle piece. Then, on page 72, use the answers to identify each person.

Top:

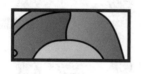

$$\begin{array}{r} 693 \\ \times\ \ 3 \\ \hline \end{array}$$

$$\begin{array}{r} 748 \\ \times\ \ 9 \\ \hline \end{array}$$

$$\begin{array}{r} 681 \\ \times\ \ 2 \\ \hline \end{array}$$

Middle:

$$\begin{array}{r} 398 \\ \times\ \ 1 \\ \hline \end{array}$$

$$\begin{array}{r} 544 \\ \times\ \ 5 \\ \hline \end{array}$$

$$\begin{array}{r} 210 \\ \times\ \ 7 \\ \hline \end{array}$$

Bottom:

$$\begin{array}{r} 999 \\ \times\ \ 4 \\ \hline \end{array}$$

$$\begin{array}{r} 823 \\ \times\ \ 8 \\ \hline \end{array}$$

$$\begin{array}{r} 498 \\ \times\ \ 3 \\ \hline \end{array}$$

Face Puzzles — Part 2

Write the correct name below each set of answers.

Graham

Libby

Alicia

1.

6,732
398
1,494

2.

2,079
1,470
6,584

_____   _____

3.

1,362
2,720
3,996

_____

Dividing Fractions: Problem Solving

Solve each problem.

1. Mrs. Anderson's class is 60 minutes long. She wants to divide her class time into 3 equal sections. How long will each section be?

2. For his math test, Zach must figure out how many days there are in 72 hours. What would the correct answer be?

_____

_____

3. Grant's science experiment on decomposition says it takes 1,460 days to complete. How many years is that?

4. Mackenzie will be in third grade in 48 months. How many years will it be until she is a third grader?

_____

_____

Climbing to the Top

Start at the bottom of the stairs. Find the quotient for the first problem, and then use it as the divisor for the next step. Repeat until you reach the top.

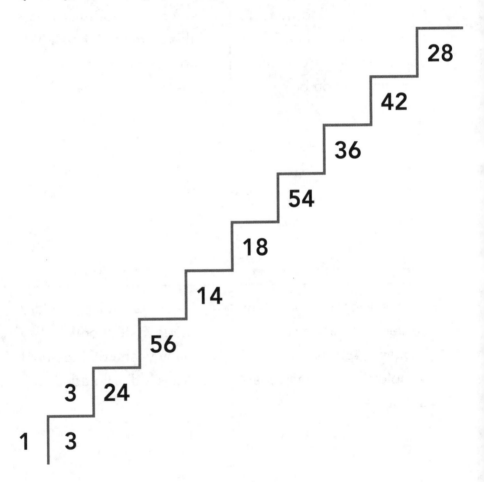

28

42

36

54

18

14

56

3 | 24

1 | 3

What's the Operation?

Choose the operation. Solve the problem.

1. Juan has $3.67 to spend at the store. His friend Edgar has $6.25. How much do they have altogether?

2. Simone and the student council have collected 492 pounds of food for local families in need. If she divides the food equally between 6 families, how much food will each family receive?

3. Recently, $\frac{1}{3}$ of the students at Washington Elementary School had perfect scores on a test. An additional $\frac{1}{4}$ of the students performed almost as well. What fraction of the students scored well on the test?

4. Zoe found out that there were 6 groups in her science class. Each group was composed of 7 students. How many students were there in all?

5. Ginny and Terrance have a great idea! They plan to save a total of $50.00 to buy clothing for the local shelter in their city. Right now they have a total of $36.89. How much more do they need to save to reach their goal?

6. Lee and Shauna are excited about the drive that they promoted at their school to support hungry children. Generous fifth and sixth graders at their school donated a total of $214.55 to the drive. The girls just found out that the department store near the school will add 6 times the total of what they collected. How much will the department store be contributing?

Answer Key

Page 3

×	1	2	3	4	5	6
1	1	2	3	4	5	6
2	2	4	6	8	10	12
3	3	6	9	12	15	18
4	4	8	12	16	20	24
5	5	10	15	20	25	30
6	6	12	18	24	30	36

1. Itself; 2. All end in even numbers.;
3. All end in 5 or 0.; 4. Even.;
5. 12

Page 4

×	7	8	9	10	11	12
7	49	56	63	70	77	84
8	56	64	72	80	88	96
9	63	72	81	90	99	108
10	70	80	90	100	110	120
11	77	88	99	110	121	132
12	84	96	108	120	132	144

1. 9; 2. 0; 3. The number appears twice in the product.

Page 5
1. 18 × (0 × 6); 2. (6 × 3) × 4;
3. 8 × (7 × 6); 4. (6 × 12) × 12;
5. 6 × (7 × 4); 6. (9 × 5) × 5;
7. 0 × (4 × 6); 8. 5 × (6 × 9);
9. 241 × (1 × 1); 10. (9 × 4) × 3;
11. (3 × 12) × 10

Page 6
1. 15, 15; 2. 6, 6; 3. 10, 10;
4. 21, 21; 5. 33, 33: 6. 18, 18;
7. 24, 24; 8. 14, 14; 9. 30, 30;
10. 16, 16; 11. 60, 60

Page 7
1. 300; 2. 400; 3. 500; 4. 600;
5. 400; 6. 600; 7. 800; 8. 1,000;
9. 1,200; 10. 900; 11. 1,200;
12. 1,500; 13. 1,800; 14. 2,100

Page 8
Estimates will vary.
1. 108; 2. 287; 3. 116; 4. 192; 5. 225;
6. 315; 7. 564; 8. 672; 9. 963;
10. 1,030; 11. 3,280

Page 9
1. 48; 2. 22; 3. 26; 4. 39; 5. 14; 6. 33;
7. 28; 8. 36; 9. 44; 10. 69; 11. 13;
12. 66; 13. 66; 14. 64; 15. 88

Page 10
1. 133; 2. 161; 3. 322; 4. 259; 5. 504;
6. 168; 7. 736; 8. 664; 9. 376; 10. 756;
11. 243; 12. 810; 13. 513; 14. 675

Page 11
1. 2,488; 2. 496; 3. 900; 4. 849
5. 1,001; 6. 645; 7. 824; 8. 750
9. 1,998; 10. 548; 11. 927; 12. 832
13. 3,609; 14. 840; 15. 756; 16. 1,200

Page 12
1. 6,000; 2. 9,000; 3. 8,440; 4. 6,042;
5. 12,630; 6. 6,290; 7. 8,164;
8. 30,720; 9. 13,628; 10. 25,563

Page 13
1. 3,372 miles; 2. 11,500 yards;
3. 294 miles; 4. 5,082 miles; 5. 455
miles; 6. Tony: 2,911 miles; Patrick:
2,368 miles

Answer Key

Page 14
1. 1,960; 2. 444; 3. 3,367; 4. 2,176;
5. 1,247; 6. 1,992; 7. 312; 8. 768;
9. 345; 10. 414; 11. 1,768; 12. 1,032

Page 15
1. 44,362; 2. 4,380; 3. 35,250;
4. 20,440; 5. 17,493; 6. 1,500;
7. 18,642; 8. 11,340; 9. 4,064;
10. 29,043; 11. 5,992; 12. 21,033

Page 16
1. 40,000; 2. 60,000; 3. 240,000;
4. 360,000; 5. 150,000; 6. 240,000;
7. 210,000; 8. 320,000; 9. 124,148;
10. 124,499; 11. 34,160; 12. 148,274;
13. 506,678; 14. 86,336; 15. 187,124;
16. 187,145

Page 17
1. 623,200; 2. 1,578,600;
3. 1,136,800; 4. 1,024,400;
5. 559,612; 6. 709,120; 7. 659,804;
8. 522,468; 9. 2,587,902;
10. 663,896; 11. 542,808;
12. 1,472,526

Page 18
1. 4,393; 2. 191; 3. 3,141; 4. 2,795;
5. 382; 6. 5,590; 7. 5,730

Page 19
1. 276; 2. 52; 3. 3,619; 4. 1,630;
5. 6,097; 6. 1,044; 7. 21,607;
8. 18,432; 9. 24,573; 10. 32,585;
11. 157,008; 12. 566,374;
13. 5,475 sit-ups; 14. 37,800 calories

Page 20
1. 8; 2. 2; 3. 5; 4. 2; 5. 7; 6. 4; 7. 0;
8. 1; 9. 5; 10. 9; 11. 3; 12. 8; 13. 9;
14. 7; 15. 6; 16. 12 bags of leaves;
17. 4 new songs

Page 21
1. 9; 2. 5; 3. 4; 4. 8; 5. 0; 6. 4; 7. 8;
8. 5; 9. 7; 10. 9; 11. 8; 12. 4; 13. 9;
14. 4; 15. 7; 16. 8; 17. 6; 18. 3

Page 22
1. 2; 2. 3; 3. 4; 4. 1; 5. 0; 6. 5; 7. 3;
8. 3; 9. 6; 10. 5; 11. 7; 12. 9; 13. 3;
14. 8; 15. 5

Page 23
1. 2; 2. 3; 3. 2; 4. 1; 5. 6; 6. 4

Page 24
1. 3; 2. 4; 3. 6; 4. 7; 5. 8; 6. 9;
7. 8; 8. 3

Page 25
1. 6; 2. 7; 3. 15; 4. 16; 5. 11;
6. 8; 7. 12; 8. 32; 9. 13; 10. 17

Page 26
1. 1 R1; 2. 2 R2; 3. 3 R1; 4. 3 R1;
5. 1 R4; 6. 2 R2

Page 27
1. 178 R1; 2. 243 R3; 3. 164 R3;
4. 69 R3; 5. 62 R5; 6. 73 R7

Page 28
1. 714 R1; 2. 922 R3; 3. 1,028 R2;
4. 4,308 R1; 5. 931 R1; 6. 1,608 R1;
7. 625 R2; 8. 244 R3; 9. 869 R7

Page 29
1. 15 snakes; 2. 851 pounds of
birdseed; 3. 83 pounds of food;
4. 210 people

Answer Key

Page 30
1. 2 R12; 2. 2 R1; 3. 1 R6; 4. 2 R10;
5. 2; 6. 1 R8; 7. 1 R10; 8. 1 R1;
9. 3 R10; 10. 4; 11. 1 R1; 12. 1 R8

Page 31
1. 9 R27; 2. 31 R15; 3. 4 R22;
4. 18 R19; 5. 23 R11; 6. 7 R2;
7. 1 R61; 8. 7 R82; 9. 15 R35;
10. 20 R15; 11. 16 R8; 12. 35 R12

Page 32
1. 13 R78; 2. 52 R1; 3. 92 R92;
4. 46 R40; 5. 83 R9; 6. 69 R11;
7. 91 R59; 8. 79 R16; 9. 55 R26

Page 33
1. 13 human years; 2. 16 years, 6;
3. 8 human years, 8; 4. 121 weeks

Page 34
1. 24; 2. 5 R4; 3. 78 R4; 4. 284;
5. 602; 6. 620; 7. 4 R3; 8. 647 R3;
9. 3 R18; 10. 9 R45; 11. 37 R53;
12. 220 R36; 13. 139 containers;
14. 281 groups

Page 35
1. 0.20; 2. 0.35; 3. 0.275; 4. 19.89;
5. 4.38; 6. 0.147; 7. 0.21; 8. 0.0396;
9. 95.13; 10. 0.558; 11. 0.5733;
12. 0.2625

Page 36
1. 0.6; 2. 6; 3. 60; 4. 43; 5. 430;
6. 4,300; 7. 653; 8. 10.9; 9. 213;
10. 46; 11. 460; 12. 0.045; 13. 3

Page 37
1. 2.4; 2. 2.7; 3. 0.84; 4. 39.2; 5. 13.5;
6. 11.24; 7. 8.8; 8. 18.18; 9. 11.2;
10. 18.6; 11. 18.5; 12. 0.68

Page 38
1. $35.00; 2. $32.00; 3. $24.00;
4. $18.00; 5. $4.00; 6. $18.00;
7. $7.00; 8. $63.00; 9. $24.00;
10. $48.00; 11. $9.00; 12. $16.00

Page 39
1. 0.28; 2. 0.15; 3. 0.324; 4. 15.66;
5. 5.04; 6. 0.084; 7. 0.18; 8. 0.0264;
9. 117.81; 10. 0.405; 11. 0.4344;
12. 0.4002; 13. 1.485; 14. 1.56;
15. 39.216; 16. 16.275

Page 40
1. 0.00182; 2. 0.000504; 3. 0.00387;
4. 0.001749; 5. 0.00244; 6. 0.0132;
7. 0.0194; 8. 0.003901; 9. 0.02781

Page 41
1. 63.65 mL; 2. 56.096 mL;
3. 136.8 cm; 4. 0.63 kg

Page 42
1. 1.26; 2. 0.42; 3. 0.1032; 4. 2.7004;
5. 0.063; 6. 0.03; 7. 0.1435;
8. 0.02778; 9. 0.243; 10. 1.778;
11. 76.36; 12. 0.00186;
13. 67 ounces; 14. 0.036 miles

Answer Key

Page 43
1. 0.54; 2. 1.15; 3. 0.95; 4. 0.0775;
5. 1.62; 6. 1.575; 7. 0.838; 8. 0.748;
9. 13.35; 10. 0.535; 11. 1.34; 12. 0.325

Page 44
1. 0.62, 0.062, 0.0062;
2. 52.53, 5.253, 0.5253;
3. 105.09, 10.509, 1.0509;
4. 9.0565, 0.90565, 0.090565

Page 45
1. 0.3; 2. 0.03; 3. 0.23; 4. 0.023;
5. 22.7; 6. 2.27; 7. 4.91; 8. 0.021;
9. 20.1

Page 46
1. 9; 2. 0.2; 3. 9.9; 4. 0.8; 5. 6.2; 6. 7;
7. 0.5; 8. 0.8; 9. 3

Page 47
1. $0.66/pound; 2. $0.42 each;
3. $0.22/ounce; 4. $0.04/cup

Page 48
1. 0.9; 2. 0.42; 3. 0.23; 4. 2.14;
5. 8.03; 6. 5.07; 7. 0.009; 8. 0.0063;
9. 0.08; 10. 2.3; 11. 230; 12. 36;
13. $0.27/ounce; 14. 10.6 feet

Page 49
1. $7\frac{1}{2}$; 2. $1\frac{3}{4}$; 3. $2\frac{6}{7}$; 4. $8\frac{3}{5}$; 5. $2\frac{7}{8}$; 6. $4\frac{1}{5}$;
7. $2\frac{7}{12}$; 8. $2\frac{1}{2}$; 9. $1\frac{5}{8}$; 10. $2\frac{3}{4}$; 11. $5\frac{4}{9}$;
12. $6\frac{5}{6}$; 13. $7\frac{2}{3}$; 14. $11\frac{1}{4}$; 15. 12; 16. $3\frac{2}{7}$;
17. 12; 18. 8

Page 50
1. $\frac{7}{3}$; 2. $\frac{27}{4}$; 3. $\frac{13}{12}$; 4. $\frac{25}{8}$; 5. $\frac{38}{5}$; 6. $\frac{19}{10}$; 7. $\frac{17}{5}$;
8. $\frac{103}{11}$; 9. $\frac{27}{7}$; 10. $\frac{29}{5}$; 11. $\frac{53}{12}$; 12. $\frac{73}{11}$

Page 51
1. $\frac{1}{4}$; 2. $\frac{2}{5}$; 3. $\frac{1}{3}$; 4. $\frac{2}{3}$; 5. $\frac{1}{3}$; 6. $\frac{3}{5}$; 7. $\frac{3}{4}$;
8. $\frac{1}{12}$; 9. $\frac{2}{3}$; 10. $\frac{1}{3}$; 11. $\frac{1}{4}$; 12. $\frac{5}{6}$; 13. $\frac{1}{2}$;
14. $\frac{1}{4}$; 15. 1

Page 52
1. $\frac{2}{15}$; 2. $\frac{1}{12}$; 3. $\frac{1}{4}$; 4. $\frac{3}{8}$

Page 53
1. 2; 2. $1\frac{3}{5}$; 3. $\frac{6}{7}$; 4. $1\frac{1}{7}$; 5. $2\frac{2}{5}$; 6. $\frac{9}{10}$;
7. $6\frac{3}{4}$; 8. $1\frac{4}{5}$; 9. $1\frac{1}{3}$; 10. $1\frac{5}{7}$; 11. $\frac{3}{5}$; 12. $1\frac{1}{2}$

Page 54
1. $\frac{9}{16}$; 2. $\frac{7}{9}$; 3. $1\frac{1}{2}$; 4. $1\frac{1}{7}$; 5. $\frac{7}{8}$; 6. $2\frac{1}{10}$;
7. $1\frac{1}{3}$; 8. $3\frac{1}{2}$; 9. $1\frac{7}{12}$; 10. $\frac{5}{18}$; 11. $\frac{4}{5}$; 12. $\frac{5}{9}$;
13. $3\frac{1}{2}$; 14. $1\frac{7}{12}$; 15. $1\frac{9}{16}$

Page 55
1. $6\frac{1}{2}$; 2. $3\frac{3}{5}$; 3. $3\frac{6}{7}$; 4. $9\frac{1}{7}$; 5. $6\frac{4}{5}$; 6. $6\frac{9}{10}$;
7. $15\frac{3}{4}$; 8. $12\frac{9}{10}$; 9. $12\frac{1}{2}$; 10. $7\frac{5}{7}$; 11. $12\frac{3}{5}$;
12. $21\frac{1}{2}$; 13. $9\frac{1}{5}$; 14. $12\frac{7}{9}$; 15. $10\frac{2}{7}$

Page 56
1. 10; 2. $3\frac{1}{8}$; 3. $4\frac{19}{20}$; 4. $2\frac{3}{5}$; 5. $2\frac{6}{25}$; 6. $8\frac{1}{3}$;
7. $7\frac{1}{2}$; 8. $14\frac{7}{10}$; 9. $5\frac{13}{24}$

Page 57
1. $2\frac{2}{5}$ miles; 2. $4.00; 3. $\frac{1}{4}$; 4. $60\frac{2}{3}$ hours

Page 58
1. $\frac{5}{24}$; 2. $\frac{7}{30}$; 3. $\frac{1}{14}$; 4. $\frac{3}{10}$; 5. 6; 6. $1\frac{2}{3}$; 7. $1\frac{5}{7}$;
8. $2\frac{1}{12}$; 9. $1\frac{7}{8}$; 10. $3\frac{2}{3}$; 11. $6\frac{1}{4}$; 12. $16\frac{1}{2}$;
13. 12 hours; 14. 3 miles

Page 59
1. $\frac{5}{11}$; 2. $\frac{4}{9}$; 3. $\frac{1}{9}$; 4. $\frac{10}{3}$; 5. $\frac{7}{1}$; 6. $\frac{8}{37}$; 7. $\frac{11}{15}$;
8. $\frac{6}{1}$; 9. $\frac{4}{3}$

Page 60
1. $13\frac{1}{2}$; 2. 35; 3. $\frac{1}{14}$; 4. $6\frac{2}{3}$; 5. $\frac{1}{8}$; 6. $\frac{9}{40}$;
7. $\frac{3}{8}$; 8. $2\frac{2}{5}$; 9. $\frac{4}{15}$; 10. $\frac{5}{18}$; 11. $\frac{7}{12}$; 12. 12

Page 61
1. 7; 2. 2; 3. 2; 4. $1\frac{11}{24}$; 5. $13\frac{1}{2}$; 6. $6\frac{2}{3}$;
7. $8\frac{3}{4}$; 8. $1\frac{5}{9}$; 9. 1; 10. $\frac{1}{2}$; 11. $\frac{3}{10}$; 12. $\frac{3}{5}$;
13. 5; 14. 2; 15. $\frac{5}{6}$; 16. $\frac{3}{5}$

Answer Key

Page 62
1. $5\frac{1}{15}$; 2. $\frac{5}{6}$; 3. $1\frac{11}{19}$; 4. $\frac{11}{16}$; 5. $1\frac{4}{7}$; 6. $2\frac{1}{3}$;
7. 5; 8. $5\frac{11}{14}$; 9. $1\frac{19}{35}$; 10. $3\frac{7}{19}$; 11. 5; 12. $\frac{17}{20}$

Page 63
1. 4; 2. $1\frac{3}{4}$; 3. $1\frac{9}{25}$; 4. $\frac{3}{4}$; 5. 2; 6. $3\frac{1}{6}$;
7. $6\frac{2}{3}$; 8. $4\frac{1}{2}$; 9. $1\frac{1}{5}$; 10. $3\frac{3}{7}$; 11. 3; 12. $\frac{1}{2}$;
13. $2\frac{1}{14}$; 14. 3; 15. $\frac{5}{6}$

Page 64
1. 8 servings; 2. $6\frac{1}{2}$ ounces;
3. $1\frac{3}{4}$ pounds; 4. $\frac{3}{20}$ pound

Page 65
1. $\frac{3}{2}$; 2. $\frac{4}{7}$; 3. $\frac{2}{9}$; 4. $\frac{1}{5}$; 5. $\frac{3}{34}$; 6. 24;
7. 24; 8. 30; 9. 7; 10. $6\frac{2}{3}$; 11. $\frac{15}{16}$;
12. $\frac{10}{21}$; 13. $5\frac{1}{3}$; 14. $2\frac{3}{4}$; 15. $\frac{1}{8}$; 16. $\frac{3}{16}$;
17. $\frac{9}{20}$; 18. 5 beads; 19. 4 days

Page 66
1. 2 × 2 × 7; 2. 3 × 7;
3. prime; 4. 2 × 2 × 2 × 2 × 3

Page 67
1. 2 × 2 × 3 × 3; 2. prime;
3. 2 × 2 × 2 × 2 × 2;
4. 2 × 2 × 2 × 3;
5. prime; 6. 2 × 3 × 3;

Page 68
1. 2 × 2 × 5; 2. 2 × 5 × 5;
3. 3 × 3 × 3; 4. prime;
5. 5 × 11; 6. 2 × 3 × 7

Page 69
1. 63 ÷ 7 = 9; quotient = 9;
2. 848 ÷ 2 = 424; divisor = 2;
3. 49 ÷ 7 = 7; dividend = 49;

Page 70
1. D; 2. F; 3. A; 4. E; 5. C; 6. B

Page 71
top: 2,079; 6,732; 1,362
middle: 398; 2,720; 1,470
bottom: 3,996; 6,584; 1,494

Page 72
1. Libby; 2. Graham; 3. Alicia

Page 73
1. 20 minutes; 2. 3 days;
3. 4 years; 4. 4 years

Page 74

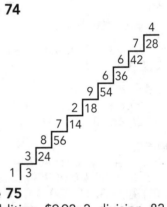

Page 75
1. addition, $9.92; 2. division, 82 lb.;
3. addition, 7/12; 4. multiplication, 42;
5. subtraction, $13.11;
6. multiplication, $1,287.30